Red Jacket And Yellow Squash

True Testimonies Of What God Can Do

Don Horne

Help Publish Me USA
Red Oak, Texas

Red Jacket
And
Yellow Squash

ISBN-13: 978-0615560090

ISBN-10: 0615560090

Published by Help Publish Me USA
http://www.helppublish.me
Red Oak, Texas

Contents

Section Four

A Very Special Testimonial

Dedication

This book is dedicated with love and appreciation to Doris McNellis for the inspiration she is to all of us as a Sunday School leader, Christian, and friend. Her testimonials of a Daddy's love in giving to his daughters are the basis for the name of the book. Her father provided answers to her prayers just as our Father, God, does for us.

It is also dedicated to my kids and grandchildren. I wanted you to know, and for you to settle it in your hearts, the awesome power of God. There are no other gods. The rest are idols of man. Keep your faith and guard your heart.

Foreword

"This is an inspiring collection of testimonies about God touching the lives of ordinary people. These stories of healing and supernatural help will lift your spirits and strengthen your faith. How encouraging to be reminded of how much God cares for His children."

~Kermit S. Bridges, D. Min

President

Southwestern Assemblies of God

University

Waxahachie, Texas

Acknowledgments

I wish to thank all the people which permitted me to contribute their testimonials to this book. I have enough coming in already to begin a second book. A book in this genre of testimonials could never have had the impact it has if it was fiction. The very fact it is a compilation of miracles and testimonials from "ordinary" people makes it particularly real and precious to me. Although, let me point out you are not ordinary. You are special and God proves it every day!

~Don Horne

The Bible Says:

"Let no negative word proceed out of your mouth, but only that which is good for the edification of the moment. So that it will grant Grace to them that hear."

Ephesians 4:29

"They overcame him (Satan) by the blood of the Lamb, and by the word of their testimony."

Revelation 12:11

How powerful are our testimonies? They are..."mighty through God to the pulling down (destruction) of strongholds!"

2 Corinthians 10:4

Section One
God's Providence

"This is the confidence we have in approaching God, that if we ask anything according to His will, He hears us. And if we know that He hears us—whatever we ask—we know that we have of Him what we asked of Him."

I John 5:14 -15

"He will be the sure foundation for your times, a rich store of salvation, wisdom, and knowledge; the fear of the Lord is the key to this treasure."

Isaiah 33:6

How can we not believe God is interested in the smallest details of our lives? We need to learn to walk knowing we have, as our birthright into the Kingdom of God, His wisdom and strength for any occasion. "The steps of a righteous man are ordered by the Lord!"

Our daily lives are as important to God as our desperate groanings in the middle of the darkest night. We have the evidence of things not seen to lead us...faith! Some of the testimonials you are getting ready to read are about people which asked God for the smallest things imaginable to the world...a red jacket, a meal of yellow squash, even a can of Black Flag Bug Spray. However, because the one praying the prayer of faith desired something, it was God's "great pleasure to give to His children."

These people were not given a stone when they asked for bread. There were not even any substitutes; God gave them what they asked.

"People ought always to pray." Pray for wisdom. Pray for guidance. Pray for your lost keys. Pray for good weather for a birthday party. Pray for a bad boss. Pray for relationships. Pray for deliverance from addictions. Get the picture? God is interested in anything that concerns you.

Red Jacket and Yellow Squash

Doris McNellis

My parents divorced when I was twelve and it broke my heart. I loved my Daddy. My mother had to contend with being a single mother, but my dad helped to support us until we were out of high school.

After graduation I went to Southwestern Assemblies of God University in Waxahachie, Texas, and Daddy was to come one Fall Saturday to buy school clothes for my Freshman sister. The only coat I had was a heavy fur coat, and I wanted a light jacket to wear between classes and on campus. I prayed to God about Him providing one for me, preferably red.

My daddy came and invited me to go shopping with him and my sister. I was overjoyed to be with Daddy. He always liked to go to El Fenix, which was a great Mexican restaurant at the time in downtown Dallas. Afterward, we went shopping. As my dad shopped for my sister, I stood admiring a display of the very jacket for which I had prayed to God. It was red and not very heavy.

My Daddy saw me looking, and asked me to try on the jacket. "Do you like it, Sis? Does it fit?"

"Oh, yes, Daddy!" I replied.

"Well, I think we will just get that for you."

I could not believe God picked out the very coat I had prayed to Him about, and allowed my beloved Daddy to give it to me!

*****

One day I had a tremendous craving for yellow squash. I prayed to God in my daily prayers about me finding enough yellow squash for a meal. A couple which I had never met, and who had recently moved in down the street from me, came by that very afternoon and left me a bag of fresh garden vegetables on my porch. When I came home I took the bag into the house.

I emptied the bag of different vegetables and at the very bottom was.....enough yellow squash for a meal! For the squash to be at the bottom of the bag, it would have to have been put in first! This may seem small to some people, but the fact God would be interested in the most minute details of our lives caused me to pause and praise Him!

*****

Prayed For Black Flag

Wanda Jones

With not a lot of money as a single parent to buy extras such as bug killer, I prayed to God to help me get a can of Black Flag Bug Spray to help me kill some bugs.

After praying I was standing out by the curb at the edge of my yard. The street made a curve right in front of my house. While I was there a big truck came by and something fell off the back. I looked down and a can of Black Flag Bug Spray came rolling right up to my feet! God's Providence and timing are awesome!

*****

Chance To Witness By Returning Bible

Wanda Jones

I have a vacant house in Balch Springs, Texas, and one Saturday I went over to check on the house. As I drove up I saw something lying in front of the fence next to the street. I got out and went and picked it up. It was a very nice Bible. I opened it and there were some names written in it.

I came home and opened my phone book and called one of the names. A lady answered and was very happy. She told me someone had stolen their truck on Friday. Her husband said he did not care about the truck, and what he wanted was the Bible. She had given it to him when they were dating. The Bible had been laying on the dashboard of the truck.

They came to retrieve the Bible. I don't

remember how long she said they had been married, but they wanted a baby so bad. I was able to lay hands on them and pray for God to give them a baby. He did. God works in mysterious ways.

*****

Returned Wallet

One day I went to Wal Mart in Mesquite on Highway 30. As I drove in the parking lot, I saw a billfold lying in the street. I stopped my car, got out, and went and picked it up. It had over 400 dollars in it. I went into the store and told them I had found a billfold on the lot. If anyone came looking for it to have them call me, and I left my phone number.

I came home and tried looking in the billfold for a name or something to see if I could find the owner. I found a Sears charge card. I called Sears, but they said they could not help me. I kept looking in phone books until I found one listed in Garland with that name.

I called and the lady which answered the phone was crying. I asked her what was wrong and she said, "We lost everything we own." I asked her what, and she said, "It was a billfold with all our money in it." I told her not to worry that I had it. However, I told her I lived all the way in Seagoville. She said that her husband had gone to Wal Mart and when he came back they would come and get it.

They came to my house to get the billfold, and hugged and kissed me, and hugged and kissed me! They were ill, and it must have been because they had lost their billfold after just cashing their check.

*****

Car On Fire

A neighbor of mine was in Baylor Hospital, and her niece wanted to go see her. So, I drove the niece's car to Dallas to Baylor Hospital. On our way home from the hospital on Highway 175, I looked and the car next to me was on fire! I asked her where was the horn and that the car next to us was on fire. She would not tell me where the horn was.

She just kept saying, "Go on and get out of here!"

I kept trying to get her to tell me, but she would not. I kept trying to find the horn and finally I pushed on the turn signal and it blew the horn. However, the two ladies in the car did not hear me. So, I drove fast, got in front of them, and drove slow while I motioned for them to pull over. When they stopped I said, "Your car is on fire!"

They got out and started running, but the fire went out. They came back to the car and the older woman said to the driver, "I told you not to run over that recliner!"

I told the lady who was driving to get in the car and put it in reverse and back up very slowly. The other lady and I stood on the chair and mashed it down and it came free! They hugged and kissed me. It was the metal on the chair that had the whole bottom of the car on fire. If it would have reached the gas tank they would not be here!

*****

What I Wanted In A Man

Cleta Bell

In June 1978 I found myself praying my heart out for the second time in three years. My oldest son, Melvin, had been murdered by a hitchhiker he picked up trying to help. My husband of 26 years had left me for a younger woman 2 ½ years prior.

I was lying on my bed crying my eyes out with a broken heart. I was so devastated I could barely function. I had lost so much weight from not eating or sleeping that I was passing out at work. The doctor where I worked ordered me to come to his office. He gave me a very strong talk and a B12 shot. He told me to live my life with great pride and to start going out on dates if asked.

I lay on my bed crying out to God for help. My prayer was, "Lord, I will stay single the rest of my life if that is what you want, and not fall out with you. However, I am still young (I was 47) and I would really like a Christian companion. You pick for me. Not one that I would pick. Then I listed five things I wanted in a man:

1. I wanted him to fall in love with my spirit first.
2. I wanted him to be my spiritual leader.
3. I wanted him to love my kids as his own.
4. I wanted him to need a home, because I had a house to share.
5. He could even be younger than me, because I am young at heart.

I told the Lord it was in His hands and I left it at that. I went on a singles retreat over the weekend and had a great time with others like me and with the Lord.

About in July, a friend of mine, Francis, told me Doug Bell was divorced from his wife and Doris, his friend, was trying to get him to go to our singles class. Those two got us together on a

Sunday night after church. I did not think much about it until I was told he wanted to see me again.

The first date we had, he stuck his head in my car window and said, "Cleta, I have never seen you before in my life, but my Spirit is drawn to yours." That was number <u>one</u> on my list! A few dates later I found out through his divorce he had given his ex-wife his house; number four on my list!

He <u>adored</u> my kids as he had none of his own. Number three on my list!

He <u>is</u> my Spiritual leader, The Lord gets all the Glory for this as he lived in Lewisville, and I lived in Lancaster, 45 miles from one another. He went to church in Desoto, and I went to Beverly Hills; also miles apart. We went together almost nine months, and we were married April 7, 1979. My son married us, my daughter in law was bridesmaid, and my three year old granddaughter was my flower girl. We will be married 33 years in April 2012!

Section Two

God's Healing

Most of the next group of testimonials are about healing. Some are absolutely miraculous, but all are from a loving, all powerful God.

In the story of Jesus raising Lazarus from the dead I have always loved the short verse, "Jesus wept." He knew He was going to heal Lazarus, but seeing the grief and despair touched Him. That fact of the love of Jesus should not be lost on anyone needing comfort. God cares!

"By faith in the name of Jesus, this man whom you see and know was made strong. It is Jesus' name and the faith that comes through Him, that has given this complete healing to him, as you all can see."

Acts 3:16

Peter and John had just healed a lame man which had been lame since birth, and the people were astounded and looked on them as if it was something which was done through them and fleshly power. Peter was quick to point out the "God of Abraham, Isaac, and of Jacob, the God of our fathers, hath glorified His son, Jesus."

Peter made sure the people knew where the healing came from—Jesus' name and the faith which comes from knowing and calling out that name.

As glorious as these testimonials are about healing, and, in the natural realm they are supernatural, remember this, in the Heavenly Realm, the supernatural is the natural!

There Is Nothing Too Big For My God!

Wanda Jones

Wanda Jones is the mother of Charlotte Heilaman, a member of Doris' Sunday School Class at The Oaks Fellowship in Red Oak, Texas. *"She is 82, wears high heels, and still cuts her own yard. She is a mighty prayer warrior and people call her to pray all the time. My father passed away when I was 13, and she raised us three girls on Faith because we sure didn't have any money. We didn't really get to participate in extracurricular activities at school because we knew the money just wasn't there. But, God provided our every need and I wouldn't take anything for that lesson. We learned early in life through experience that we could trust him for anything we needed and it made us strong."* (Charlotte's description.)

Healing For Grandson's Foot

Wanda Jones

About five or so years ago, my grandson tried jumping across something and broke his foot. He was not living for Jesus. They called me and on the way to the hospital the song "Victory" kept rolling over and over in my mind.

I got to the hospital and they told me I could go see him but only one person at a time could be in the room. I walked into the room and started to tell my daughter she would have to go out for a minute while I visited him. I looked and saw his foot, turned, and ran out of the room! It was horrible! His foot was turned completely sideways, and blood was coming out. I went outside and prayed fervently. Yes, I even spoke in tongues over my grandson.

The doctor said he was going to have to operate in about two hours and put pins in his ankle. We anointed my grandson with oil and prayed in the name of Jesus.

When the doctor came back from surgery, he said, "I did not have to use pins. I just had to pop it back into place! However, he cannot put any weight on his foot for six months."

The following Sunday I went to the church his mother attends in Dallas, and he came to the service on crutches in terrible pain in his foot. The church was having a miracle service that morning, and had been fasting and praying.

Some of the members were asked to bring loaves of bread to distribute to people who wanted to be prayed for if they wanted a miracle. My grandson took a slice of bread, ate it, and got in the miracle line. After being prayed for he came back to his seat.

The Evangelist came down the aisle and asked, "Was anyone's teeth filled?"

My grandson exclaimed, "Oh, my God! I have two, no three, no <u>five</u> teeth filled, and I am not in any pain!"

The five fillings in his teeth were gold! He never walked on the crutches again, and he is a big, healthy man today!

*****

Baby Brought Back To Life

Wanda Jones

My daughter, Charlotte, and her husband, Scott, had purchased a new van, and a friend of mine had given me some carpet samples. Charlotte came and we were fixing to go out and pick out some mats for her van.

Before we went out Charlotte saw a skirt of mine and said, "That's pretty." I told her she could have it. She folded it and put it on a chair.

We went to my back yard to get the carpet for her mats. We went through all the samples and just as we loaded them back in the shed I heard a scream. I said, "Oh! Some kid has gotten run over!"

We went to the front yard and someone said, "Call an ambulance Jimmie has run over his daughter!"

Heather was about three years old. Charlotte and I ran over there and began praying in tongues. Her daddy, Jimmy, had his arms out holding her.

He was staring into space. She was not breathing and I believe she was dead. We kept praying. I held her and was going to kiss her and she started crying!

The ambulance came and took her to Parkland. At Parkland the doctors said she had to have bad broken bones and head injuries. We were still praying.

Her grandmother came and when she got there she was so upset because Heather's mother had on shorts. The grandmother's sister had just given her a dress. She sent her husband out to get the dress for her daughter to put on.

Back at home they had called a prayer meeting at the church and a friend had come to my house that lived out of town. She had on blue jeans and she wanted to go to the prayer meeting. I gave her the skirt I had given Charlotte for her to put on to go the prayer meeting. We stayed all night praying at the hospital. The next morning they said there were no head injuries or even broken bones! I believe she was dead and God brought her back to life because we prayed, and He healed the head injuries and broken bones! That is not all the story.

The neighbor's son in law was the one that had put Heather in her dad's arms. He was an atheist. His name was John and all night he sat on my front porch talking about what he had witnessed. The next morning he told his mother in law that as he stood there with Charlotte and me praying in tongues and God healed that baby, it made a believer out of him. He got saved that night and later became a Spirit filled Sunday School teacher! I put the part in about the skirt and the dress to tell how God arranged clothing for them. He is always one step ahead of us!

Judy Brown, who is the mother of Heather, told us on Facebook that Heather is now a beautiful, perfect mother at 29, and has a beautiful 9 year old of her own! God is good!~Editor

Healed Broken Feet

Wanda Jones

About four years ago, I went into my back yard to clean the flower bed on my patio. The children next door had been out there climbing on the bricks, and they had knocked a wall of bricks off into the flower bed.

It had about 10 bricks on it. I picked it up to take it out of the flower bed and one of the bricks fell off and broke my big toe on my left foot. Another one fell off and broke my right foot right in the middle of the foot. That was on a Saturday morning. By Sunday morning I could hardly hobble across the floor.

I go to the Seago Manor Nursing home every Sunday morning to minister. I called one of the ladies that go with us to minister and told her I could not go I had broken my toe and my foot. At about 5 minutes till 10 I was in so much pain I thought, "I will go and see if I can find something I can put on it to relieve the pain." As I got to the vanity of my bathroom, immediately, I felt the healing virtue go thru my body! I looked at my big, black, swollen toe on my left foot, and it had gone down to normal and was not black.

I looked at my swollen, red, right foot, it had gone down to normal and was not red. I reached and felt of my right foot and it felt tender for a few minutes. It was not red, but the brick had left a black line across my foot. And the left toe had a red dot where it was hit. I went that afternoon to my niece's home, and played baseball with them!

I talked to my friend's sister that was there at the nursing home service that day, and she said that was the exact time they went to prayer for me at the nursing home! God answered those people's prayer, and sent the healing virtue about six miles to my home! <u>I AM SO GLAD I KNOW WHO JESUS IS!</u>

Grandson Quit Breathing

Charlotte Heilaman

Charlotte wrote: "*Red Jacket and Yellow Squash.....Ms. Doris. Great title for a book!*"

I actually have a couple of testimonies I want to submit. One is about my grandson and how the Lord healed him. He developed epiglottitis when he was 9 months old and stopped breathing and was without oxygen for quite a while. Long story short, paramedics took him to a local hospital and when they got to the hospital, my daughter said they could not get any readings on vitals. They then careflighted him to Children's Hospital. He was in a medically induced coma for two weeks and when they brought him out of his coma, they weren't sure what damage had been done from him being without oxygen so long, but he is fine today! There are other miracles the Lord worked through the whole episode. One, there wasn't anyone at the first hospital to do an emergency tracheotomy, and there happened to be a specialist visiting his mother at the hospital who did the trache to open up his air passage. That doctor is a specialist in Dallas. God is always near!"

*****

Healed Of Snake Bite

Margret Butts

My first husband worked as an engineer. He had also been in the Air Force. We were married for several years and he was working as an engineer for a soda fountain company. I had already had one child, and I was pregnant at this time.

He got sick at work and began to bleed internally. They rushed him to the hospital in Highland Park, Illinois, where we were living. They gave him 27 pints of blood. They realized that it was service related and they rushed him over to the Veteran's Hospital. He was operated on twice, but he did not pull through the second operation.

While all this was happening, my sister came to visit and I was doing "normal" things not knowing what was going on. I went in the garage where my hamper was to do the washing. I did not turn on the light, but just raised the lid. When I put my hand into the hamper there was a coiled snake and I was bitten. My sister ran and got the iodine and put it on the bite not knowing it was the worst thing we could have done.

I called my primary care doctor and he told me just to go onto bed that it was probably a grass snake. However, he did not know it was a rattlesnake! My arm began swelling and my brother, Ted, said, "Nothing doing. I am taking you to the hospital!" It was the same hospital where my husband was at that time.

We arrived at the hospital and they lanced the swelled area and gave me an injection of HCH but nothing seemed to be helping. They did not expect me to live, or my baby survive, because the poison was headed to my heart and there were a lot of other complications that had arisen.

A woman that I knew, Darlene, came to the hospital and asked me if I knew Jesus and could she pray for me. I did not know about Jesus, but I did let her pray. She was a singer in the Baptist church, but she had received the Holy Spirit just the night before. She began praying and singing in tongues and I thought, "That is so strange. She is singing and praying in another language."

But then she started praying in English and it was so wonderful! She prayed that I would be alright, and the baby would be alright.

Because my husband had died, they let me spend the night in the hospital. I went home the next day and six months later I had the most beautiful baby girl ever! She was not red and wrinkled at all! She had beautiful, smooth, "peaches and cream" skin from the moment of birth.

That was my first experience with the power of God and the manifestation of His Spirit. When I dedicated the baby to the Lord, I invited all my unsaved relatives. Darlene sang "My God Is Real." He is!

Healed of A Stroke

Winston Sewell

In 2008 I was working and after feeling pains in my chest I knew I was having a stroke. My wife, JoAnn, immediately called Doris and some of the members of our Home Group. We called 911 and we also called Brother Tom Wilson, our pastor.

Brother Wilson was ending a meeting with a group of pastors and he had all of them pray for me. I had been unconscious at one point and on the way to the hospital I came to. By the time we got to the hospital I was feeling fine. The doctors ran tests and could not even find evidence I had had a stroke! They kept me five days in the hospital to see if it would happen again, but they sent me home. I have worked for the past three years without experiencing anything like a stroke!

Healed Through Prayer And Her Parents' Love

Dr. Peggy A. Buckner

When our daughter Nancy was born, she was diagnosed with having Goldenhar Syndrome. Symptomatic of the disease, she had tumors on both eyes greatly hindering her sight. Her joints were not formed properly. She was also diagnosed as having scoliosis.

After many doctors' visits, and even more tests, we were given the grim prognosis. She would be a vegetable. She would never have a normal childhood. She would be paralyzed, mentally retarded...severely impaired.

We were in shock, but we knew enough to call on the name of the Lord. The doctors designed a body brace to help her stay in a position to facilitate growth of joints. Every day we exercised her arms and legs, and stood on God's Word. We still went to visit the doctors, who gave us no hope, but our hope was not in them. Our hope was in Jesus Christ.

We kept working with her. As she grew, the body brace had to be changed. Intermittently, we would take her out of her brace and put her on the floor. We would move her legs and arms as if she were crawling. At about 10 months, she was crawling on her own – not very well, but she could move on her own.

At one year, we had her up teaching her how to walk. Rather than walking, when she got her balance she was running. At the age of three, we put her in her first race. She came in first place out of 25 other children in her category! Praise God!

At the age of five years, she had surgery on both eyes. She wears eyeglasses, but can see very well. She graduated from high school and college with honors! Today she is a beautiful woman working hard in a Christian-based non-profit agency, "changing the lives of children" as she puts it. To God be the glory!

*****

Cancer Healed

John Shearer

In 1997 I received a call from Charliene, a family friend, who was trying to locate my dad who was her pastor. She and her husband had served as associate pastors with him, and she had great faith in his prayers. Charliene had found a lump in her breast, and a biopsy had established that it was malignant. My dad was on vacation and could not be reached. I offered to pray for her on Sunday, before her operation on the following Wednesday.

Post-operative examination revealed the lump was no longer there! Charliene is still cancer free. Each year she goes early to her annual wellness check so that she can witness to the cancer patients about her miracle while sitting in the doctor's waiting room!

In April 2007, I received a call from Charliene. She had been taken to the ER due to severe back pain. The ER doctor suspected the pain was due to blocked arteries, and discussed a heart catherization. Charliene went into cardiac arrest, and arrangements were being made for heart bypass surgery. She asked me to pray for a miracle. She wanted healing and no surgery. I prayed with her and tests the following day established that her arteries were free and clear of any plaque. Surgery was canceled and she returned home praising God for her miracle!

In February 2011, Charliene again called for prayer. Doctors had discovered a growth in her colon the size of a golfball. Doctors were 90% certain it was cancerous. We again agreed that God's Word is true, and His promises are "yes" and "amen." Charliene and I asked for a miracle. The growth was removed, and test results again established it was not malignant!

Willie is Charliene's sister. Doctors found a large growth on her liver. Charliene brought Willie home with her following a biopsy. I received a call to pray for a miracle. We prayed, and Willie believed she was healed and insisted on another CAT scan. The mass could not be found!

*****

Saved, Healed, and Set Free

Wanda Jones

Several years ago I met a young man named Lackey who was in the Seago Manor Nursing Home. He wore house shoes all the time and walked on tippy toes. One Sunday morning he got saved during our service.

A few weeks later as I arrived at the home to gather people for our service, he had two ladies visiting him. I said, "Lackey, it is time for church."

I asked the ladies if they were kin to him, and one said she was his mother and the other one was his sister. I asked would it be alright if we took him next door to the church and baptized him. They looked at me funny. I said, "You do know he got saved and healed, don't you?"

"No, but that must have been when he called us for some shoes."

They went on to say, "By all means take him

and baptize him. We have been fasting and praying for him to be saved back in Arkansas. He has led a bad life. He had a car wreck and has not been able to wear shoes since that time. "

We took took him over and baptized him, and the next Sunday I did not see him. I talked to the counselor and she said after being healed he went out and went to work.

About two years later I went into the auto store in Seagoville and the man behind the counter said, "Well, hello! I haven't seen you in a while."

I said, "You are Lackey, aren't you?"

"Yes."

I said, "Man, the Lord saved you, healed you, and delivered you out of the home!"

I asked if he was in church, and he said, "Oh, yes, mam!"

What a blessed testimonial of God's power!

Delivered From Cigarettes

Wanda Jones

Years ago my brother lived with me, and he smoked three packs of cigarettes all day and night long. He slept in my living room and the smell would come right up into my bedroom. My sister and I began fasting and praying for him to be delivered.

He loved to watch all the Christian programs on television. We saw there was going to be a meeting at Souls Harbor on Palm Sunday, and we wanted to go. As we walked into the church door, the evangelist came down the stairs which were by the front door. He grabbed my brother and told him, "Man, I have got to pray for you tonight!"

The service began and the evangelist came down the aisle and picked my brother out. He asked him if he saw a light over his head, and my brother said, "Yes."

He said, "Is your name Hershel?" My brother said, "Yes."

He said, "Hershel, do you believe that Tuesday night when I was praying, your face came up before me?" My brother said, "Yes."

He asked Hershel, "Do you smoke?"

"Yes."

"Kools?"

Hershel said, "Yes."

The evangelist said, "Kool spelled backward is Look. Do you want to kick the habit?"

They took the pack of Kools and kicked it across the floor. Then he said, "Hershel, there are three doctors at a place called Parkland that are going to be amazed at you!" He named them off, and the only one I recognized was Dr. Davidson, Hershel's doctor. Upon hearing his doctor's name, down went Hershel in a clump. He was slain in the Spirit!

He lay there a long time and the evangelist went on around praying for other people. When

Hershel stood up, he told him to run across the front of the church and give him a hug. Hershel ran all the way and grabbed the evangelist and they danced in the Spirit!

He asked him what happened Tuesday night. When Hershel got home from work it took him 15 minutes to walk from his truck to my door because he could not get his breath. I put the fan on him and did everything I knew to do for him to help him breathe.

He was delivered from cigarettes that night!

My other brother had smoked for over 60 years and was in the hospital. My pastor went to the hospital and prayed for him and he was delivered.

His son smoked 3 packs a day, and had for over 45 years. My brother spent lots of time with him watching TV and ball games. So, my sister and I began to pray and fast for God to deliver my nephew.

He got a girlfriend and she wanted to move in

with him. She had two little girls. He thought if she was going to move in the house he would go outside and smoke when they were there.

He thought he would get used to going outside to smoke. He lit up and the thought hit him, "If I am not going to smoke around them I don't need to be smoking!" He put that cigarette out and it has been six years since he smoked another one! Prayer and fasting worked!

*****

God Always Knows Where We Are

-Healed On Vacation

Doug Bell

In 1998, my wife and I started for Alaska, and eight days later we crossed the border of Alaska. It was one of the greatest trips I have ever taken. Little did I know I was headed for a heart attack.

We pulled into a fuel stop, topped off with fuel and water and dumped our tanks. When I went to pay the attendant said to me, "Why don't you spend the night and leave in the morning? It's free."

We did, but when I got up the next morning I was having hard chest pains. I told Cleta to go and call 911. The paramedics were there in about three minutes. They started IV's in both hands and every time my heart would beat it shook my body so hard it felt like it was going to come out of my chest. I could not breathe and I broke out in a cold sweat. I realized that I was dying.

My wife was walking the floor and praying at the top of her voice. Each time she would pass me I tried to get hold of her, but the nurse would pull my hand back. After what seemed like a long time, I got hold of her. I began to tell her, "I love you, but this where we part company. I am dying!"

She pointed her finger in my face and said, "You are not going to die. God just told me so!"

It was like someone had thrown a bucket of hot water on me from the top of my head to the bottom of my feet. I did not know we were two and one half blocks from the only medicare facility within 200 miles!

They flew us on into Fairbanks and the doctor met us at the door. I had already had five shots of Nitro under the tongue and 5 shots of Demarol. The doctor asked me if I had any cuts or abrasions. I asked why and he said, "You are going to bleed." I went out like a light.

The next morning when I woke up my wife was holding my hand. She asked, "Do you know where you are?"

"Yes."

"Do you know what has happened to you?"

"Yes."

"Do you know where our trailer is?"

"Yes."

She said, "Honey, all the clothes I have is what I have on."

We prayed, "Lord, you have people all over the world. Just send us one. I will be glad to pay whatever they want to go and get our rig and park it behind the hospital."

The next day a young lady came bouncing into my room with a big smile and said, "Hello, I am Lonie Miller!"

I said, "Darling, I don't know you."

She said, "But I know you!"

Her sister had home schooled with my daughter in law from Dallas, Texas! I gave her my keys and the next day the truck and trailer were sitting behind the hospital!

Six days later they gave me a stress test, and I had another heart attack from the second test. The doctor sent me to Anchorage because the doctor I was supposed to have fell off his motorcycle and broke his leg. A trainee took me and did tests. That evening he came to see me and said, "You have done some bad damage to your heart. There is nothing I can do. I am going to medicate you and send you home."

I said, "No! I want to see my doctor."

The next morning a man came into my room on crutches. I asked, "Who are you?"

"I am Doctor Peterson."

That day the doctor did surgery on me and the next day he released me to go home.

The nurse asked did I get to fish and I said, "No." She brought us two big socks of Salmon and Halibut. God met every need we had. The nurse at the hospital told us if we had crossed the border into the Yukon there would not have been a doctor for a thousand miles!

*****

Family Healings

John Shearer

Betty Ashworth

I received a call from my cousin Beverly telling me that our cousin Betty had been diagnosed with cancer in the 4th stage the previous day (Thursday). I called Betty and we discussed her diagnosis. I asked Betty if she believed that God could heal her. She replied that she *knew* He could. We prayed for healing.

Years earlier, Betty had gall bladder surgery. The drain tube which drained fluids outside the body had become dislodged from the inside. Poison was spilling into her body and she knew she was dying. Betty asked God to heal her because she had 3 small children. She promised to serve Him always. A nurse came into the room as Betty was losing consciousness. She was rushed to surgery, and her husband was told that Betty had little chance of survival. From that prayer of faith, however, Betty survived to see her children become adults, and have children of their own.

Betty had been referred to an oncologist at M.D. Anderson Hospital in Houston. Her appointment was the following Monday. Betty brought her diagnosis and test results to the oncologist. The doctor promised to review them, but requested that Betty undergo testing in his facility. She was to return on Wednesday to discuss a treatment protocol.

Wednesday found her back at the oncologist. Betty was ushered into his office. He was seated at his desk on which there were two stacks of paper. One stack was the diagnosis from Betty's primary care physician, and the other stack was in-house test results.

The oncologist informed Betty that he had studied the diagnosis and test results from her primary care physician and concurred with his diagnosis. He said that the in-house tests showed there was no cancer and that something had happened between Thursday and Monday. Betty told him that she had prayer on Friday and that God healed her. The oncologist replied "that would be my guess!"

Margaret Shearer

Margaret is Betty Ashworth's mother. Margaret fell face forward and was taken to the ER. A CAT scan and a MRI showed that she had a serious skull fracture with some bruising on the brain. The ER doctors wanted to admit her to the hospital, but Margaret was determined to go home.

She told Betty to call me for prayer so she could be healed, and to buy her a pair of large, movie star style sunglasses. Margaret was vain enough that she did not want anyone to see the injuries to her face around her eyes. Betty called me and left a message. I arrived home hours later and immediately prayed that she would be healed.

I called Betty who told me that Margaret was so sure she was healed that she demanded another MRI and CAT scan. The skull fracture was gone, as were the bruises on her brain. Faith always works! She had been home two hours before I got the message to pray!

David Johnson

David was a family friend and former member of my father's congregation. He had an aneurism and had been in a coma for several days. Family members were communicating with him via hand squeezes. By Sunday, doctors were not expecting him to live through the night.

I was called to the hospital to pray for him by his wife, Winona. I prayed in agreement with his wife, and her brother and sister-in-law. David immediately gained consciousness and began talking to us. When healing flowed through David's body, it set off an alarm at the nurse's desk. They rushed in with a crash cart to find him awake.

The nurse asked him "what's going on?" and David responded "I'm just visiting with my family." At midnight David moved from ICU to a private room. The next day, he was moved to the rehab floor to begin rehabilitation.

Rebecca Ramsey

Rebecca is David's niece. She was on a special assignment for her company in New York. Rebecca began feeling as if she had the flu. The doctor gave her an antibiotic. After a second round of antibiotics, Rebecca did not feel better. Rebecca was given a chest x-ray to see if she had pneumonia. They found cancer that had metastasized from her lung throughout her body. It was diagnosed to be in the fourth stage.

Her son flew to New York to drive her home. Rebecca called her aunt, Winona Johnson and requested that she contact me for prayer. The family joined me in prayer. By the time Becky reached the Texas border, she was able to discontinue oxygen.

Rebecca's local doctor had arranged for her to be seen by an oncologist. He reviewed her x-rays and test reports and admitted her to the hospital. She was given chemotherapy that same day. Other tests were done. Afterward, the doctor told her that the chemotherapy had been unnecessary. The additional tests showed that she had no cancer. Praise God!

John Shearer is a friend of mine, and also a member of Doris' Sunday School Class. He is a great prayer warrior. He and I have prayed together and seen several healings, deliverances, and instances of God's Love and Providence.

Section Three

God's Love For Us

"Praise the Lord, O my soul, and forget not all His benefits – who forgives all your sins and heals all your diseases, who redeems your life from the pit and crowns you with love and compassion, who satisfies you with love and compassion, who satisfies your desires with good things so that your youth is renewed like the eagle's."

I did not understand how God could love each one of us special until I had grandchildren. I will have five, all girls, by the time this is printed, and I love each child special.

After retiring, my two girls, both teachers, wanted to share a salary and thus be home with their babies for a few days each week. "Since you are retired and not doing anything, would you keep our babies on days we work?" asked the girls. I was "blessed" to keep three of the granddaughters from the time they were only a few weeks old until the school year ended and they were around a year old.

London, Keziah, and Charli taught me more about keeping babies than I ever wanted to know. When my own children were growing up we both worked and we used paid baby sitters. I was barely involved in parenthood. However, I soon learned to recognize their cries from being hungry to being tired. I fed them, bathed them when they were very little, changed diapers, and kept them dressed, at least in the house.

Today, my grandchildren are each special to me, the same way you and I are special to the Father. The next testimonials are about the way God watches over us every day. Most of the time we do not realize His covering is there until something happens which makes us stop and give thanks.

Woman Gives Us Her Children

Doug Bell

Years ago a woman began coming to church where we went. The children would sit by us in church, and when it was time to go, they never wanted to go home with their mother. We found out she was doing drugs and alcohol and living with one man then another.

One day they showed up at our door with their suitcases. Their mother gave the two children to us along with Power of Attorney and everything. They were ours.

The little boy was six and the little girl was eight. They lived with us for three years while their mother gave up drugs and rehabilitated. The boy's name was Rodney, and the girl's name was Shelley.

Soon after they came, the company I worked for went bankrupt and I lost my job. I had a friend which did not know I was out of work but came by and offered me a part time job that kept us going. I would go along the roadside and pick up cans for spending money for the kids.

My last two checks from my old company had bounced and I owed the bank some money. I went to the company to see if I could get a little of the money they owed me, and when I was leaving God told me to take the back road home out of the plant. I hated that road! It was narrow and rough, but I went. I was driving slow and suddenly I noticed there were dollar bills in the grass beside the road! I stopped and picked up twenty dollar bills by the handful. It was the exact amount I needed to go to the bank!

Rodney, who called me Daddy, told me, "Daddy, I would really like a cold drink."

All I had was the money we had picked up. However, as we walked back to the truck, I found a five dollar bill by itself! God provided him a cold drink!

The children would go to church with us and worshipped with us as we praised the Lord in the Spirit. Rodney took some wood and made an altar in the garage and would have the neighborhood kids come and he would lead them to the Lord. He told me, "When God gives me the Baptism, I am going to out dance you!"

Sure enough, it wasn't long before he did get the Baptism of the Holy Spirit with the evidence of speaking in tongues. He danced all over the church, up and down the aisles, and across the front with his eyes closed the entire time! He even out danced me!

His sister, Shelley, asked me one day, "Do you think God loves me?"

"Of course He does, honey."

"Do you think He loves me enough to give me a pink bicycle with a wire basket?"

"Yes, He can." I said.

"I want a <u>red</u> bicycle with handlebar streamers!" chimed in Rodney.

That is the prayer we all prayed.

I had forgotten about it after a few days, but I received a phone call from their real father and he wanted to come and see the children. I told him to come on. When he arrived, he had a bicycle for each of them. The look on the children's faces was pure joy and astonishment!

Shelley's was pink with a wire basket, and Rodney's was bright red with red and white handlebar streamers! Their dad had the bikes for three months, but it took their prayer of faith to receive them.

After about three years their mother came by and asked if I would give her back her children. She was healed of drug addiction, and was very neatly dressed. God had told me I would have to give the kids back to her someday, but it was still sad to see them go. We lost touch for a long time.

I was at an RV show in Market Hall in Dallas years later and I kept hearing this salesman talking. I did not recognize him but the voice was familiar. When I asked him his name, he said his name was Rodney! By then he was over 30 years old and prematurely bald. We sat and talked for the longest time. He told me his sister was married and had three kids, and his mother was married and doing well.

God can do anything!

*****

Regional Basketball Tickets

Wilma Sosbe

When I was a high school freshman in Indianapolis, Indiana, (the state where basketball is supreme), I really wanted to attend the Regional Basketball Tournament where our school's team was participating. I asked my parents for money to buy a packet of tickets. No money. I then asked the Lord for some way to get tickets since He understood how important this weekend was for me.

Walking down a hallway between classes on Thursday, I looked down and saw a packet of Regional tickets. I picked them up and looked around for anyone which might have been looking for something they had dropped. The battle began: should I turn them in to Lost and Found?

They told me that if no one had claimed them by Friday afternoon I could have them. The girl on the counter told me she also had found a packet of tickets and I could have them too if no one claimed them by Friday.

Friday I could hardly concentrate on classes, and I could not wait for three o' clock. I also thought about the other packet of tickets. Butler Fieldhouse is very large, and, if I took a friend, maybe we could wave to each other during the games. When I picked up the unclaimed tickets, I discovered the location of the reserved seats were right next to each other in a great section of the fieldhouse! God is not only giving, but it is beyond our understanding and belief! He also has a great sense of humor!

*****

Let God Do The Driving

My husband and I started dating while he lived in Wisconsin and I lived in Indiana. We took turns driving to visit on weekends. It was my turn to drive to Wisconsin. After a meeting in Chicago all day, I started North at about 5 p.m. As I was driving on the highway, I needed to cross a four lane bridge. Did I mention it had been snowing and sleeting all day? However, Alan reassured me that all was clear in Wisconsin.

As I was crossing the bridge in the far left lane with a semi behind me, my Toyota began a slide across the bridge to the far right lane. I fought the wheel for control and found none. I was at the mercy of the ice. I looked to my right as the side of the bridge drew nearer to my car, and saw a glimpse of a white Being. I started laughing because He was wearing His seat belt! My car then found traction and I continued on more snow.

The return trip on Sunday provided a lovely, bright, sun shiny day with no clouds in the sky, but plenty of ice on the back roads. I had one steep hill to descend to return to the main highway. I stopped at the top of the hill to make sure I could get to the bottom where there was a STOP sign.

On the left were two cars facing each other with the hoods up and jumper cables doing their job. On the right were a car and a truck parked on the side of the road. There was enough room for me to go straight down between them all.

As I took my foot off the brake and started down, my car slid sideways. Not knowing what to do, I asked God to drive. The car continued to slide, but it turned around backward and went right between all the other vehicles! I then felt the car slide sideways once again, hit some dry pavement, and then stopped. I waved to the men up on the hill, turned, and stopped at the STOP sign. I then continued on my uneventful trip home.

A Great God Bargain

Wilma Sosebe

Years ago, before there was Handicap Parking, my mother found it difficult to walk from a long way out in the parking lot and also walking around in the store. I did the best I could to find a good place close to the door, but it did not work very well most of the time. So, I asked God for a "deal." I told Him to please give us a really close parking place whenever Mother was with me, and then whenever I was alone, I would be willing to park anywhere and make the long walks. God blessed us with excellent parking places whenever Mother was in the car, and when she was not, I got to do a lot of walking.

God And Hydroplaning

Wilma Sosebe

The construction on Highway 35 seemed to go on forever since we had moved to Dallas. They were widening both sides of the road with lanes twisting and turning in all directions other than straight.

It had been raining really hard while I was trying to get home from visiting my children in Waco. It was one of those nights you could not see very far ahead, and, no matter how fast the windshield wipers wiped, visibility was poor at best.

I came to one of these twisting, turning areas of the highway and was going 25 miles per hour less than the stated speed limit. Hydroplaning is not my favorite activity, especially next to an 18 wheeler. However, all of a sudden the car had no traction and was headed into or under the semi. As is my custom in a bad situation, I asked God to do the driving because I had no control. The thought crossed my mind that if God did NOT take control I would be seeing Him very soon!

I am still here because God set the car straight and kept it straight until I felt traction under the tires! I continued the trip home, but I know Who the best driver was that night.

Don,

There are many more items I could share, but I believe these are enough for now. I am really not a bad driver, but I believe God puts me in these situations where I know without a shadow of a doubt Who is in control of everything. These situations remind me of His great Love for me and help me to stay focused on Him.

Wilma,

Maybe so, but if we ever go anywhere together..I drive!

Don

Angel Protects Child

Dr. Peggy A. Buckner

My husband was at home with our children one day. Both children had been put down for naps. Our son, who was two at the time, awoke first. So, my husband decided to cut his hair. He took him in to the master bath to work on his hair. Unbeknownst to him, our older child woke up. She looked around the house and did not see anyone. She then went to the front door, opened it, and left the house. My husband was completely unaware.

While he was cutting our son's hair, he heard the doorbell ring. He went to the door and there stood a woman with our daughter. He was totally shocked at the recount. This lady had picked up our daughter a few blocks away from our house. Our daughter had shown the lady where we stayed and she had brought her home! We were so thankful to God. For months, we searched for this lady to show our gratitude. We could not find anyone that had ever heard of her. We know God sent an angel that day to bring our baby back home!

*****

An Answer To Prayer

Cozadene Martin

You have read the story before in St. John Chapter 11, when Martha and Mary's brother, Lazarus, died. They had sent for Jesus thinking he would come immediately while Lazarus was just sick. They were heartbroken when He arrived four days late and Lazarus had died. We all know the Glorious ending when Jesus rose him from the dead. He was actually right on time.

My story begins on May 31, 1979, when my husband, H. T. Martin, passed away from a heart attack in Lindale, Texas, where he was building a new three bedroom house on 30 acres with a lake on it. This property was across the road from David Wilkerson's ranch that he had built for young converts to live and be trained in the Bible and the work of the Lord. At this time, my husband was working for Brother Wilkerson as a security guard on the ranch.

With my husband's death, I was left with an unfinished house to be completed before I could put it on the market to sell. I will always be indebted to Dub Scott, a deacon on the church board at the time. He took his crew of men to Lindale and finished the work on the house. (Dub has already gone on to his reward.)

The heavy burden of the sale of this property was more than I could handle. I was still working on the church staff full-time, and finding it very difficult to keep my mind on my work. The bank in Duncanville renewed the note on this property twice...two six month term periods.

The last six month period was coming due on 9-13-1980, and the bank told me they could not renew the note for a third time. During this time, I had placed the property in the hands of a real estate company in Tyler, Texas. This company was not making any progress in trying to get a buyer. So, I increased my praying, and asking for prayer, that I would find a buyer before the end of the six month period to be able to pay my term loan.

I will never forget the date of 7-16-1980. While praying at the altar on Wednesday night after church, Willie Jo Taylor came over and also began praying with me. The Lord spoke through her to tell me my prayer would be answered within two months. I also requested prayer in my Sunday School Class, and my teacher, Doris McNellis, told me she could hear her husband, L.J., at four o'clock in the morning, praying and walking the hall asking God to send me a buyer.

Since the Tyler real estate company was not helping me, I contacted the *Don Nevins Real Estate Company* and explained the problem to him. I found out later Don was a relative of the Zielke family. To continue my story, on Friday, 9-12-1980, remember the due date was 9-13-1980, and unfortunately it was a Saturday and the bank would be closed! Don Nevins called me at the church and asked if I was ready to go to Tyler and sign a contract. I almost shouted right there in the office! Don picked me up and we went to Tyler, closed out the deal, and hit the freeway back to Duncanville—as fast as Don could drive. I kept asking him if he thought we could get to the bank before it closed. I can say that Don was a very good and careful driver but the Lord kept all of the highway patrolmen looking the other way.

We arrived at the bank at 4 p.m. – just two hours before it closed. I dashed into the bank and handed them a check. They gave me back my canceled note stamped Paid In Full! My prayer that night was, "God, you knew from the beginning you were going to answer my prayer. Why did you take me all the way to just two hours left?"

Though He was late...He was right on time! I have learned His ways are better than our ways.

Never Give Up

Darlene and Reverend Robert Bailey

When my husband, Robert Bailey, was a small boy in the late 1930's and early 1940's, he lived in a rural area of Louisiana near the Arkansas state line. His dad was a "sharecropper." Robert had four older siblings, two brothers and two sisters. Their parents took them to a saw mill where the people from the community gathered on Sundays to have church. A few able ministers from different denominations would take turns coming there to preach.

The mother of this family was Ethel (Duke) Bailey. She suffered with asthma and other health issues. Ethel had a very dear friend named Lutie Taylor, who also attended the church services with her family. I don't know whether Ethel realized she might not live to raise her children, but she asked her friend, Lutie, to please pray for her family to come to know the Lord if anything happened to her.

She died at age 38. Robert was four years old. After their mother's death, their father dropped out of church with his family. Robert does remember hearing his dad praying in the night many times.

He continued to raise his children alone until he died at age 49. Robert was 16 years old. The other siblings were grown and Robert would live with different family members for a while.

The summer of his 16th year, teenagers, who attended the Assembly of God Church, invited him to go to youth camp. He went and was saved during the last service on Friday night. He then began attending the Assembly of God Church. He was the only one from his family to attend church for many years.

While he was still in high school, he decided to transfer to Southwestern Bible Institute, now Southwestern Assembly of God University, SAGU, in Waxahachie, Texas. They had a high school then as well as a college. I am sure his pastor had some influence in that decision.

Robert graduated from high school and attended college for a couple of years. He would hitchhike to Louisiana and back when he got "homesick." Usually he lived in the boys' dorm or lived with a local pastor.

After we were married he accepted an invitation to pastor a small country church in Arkansas near where he grew up. We were there about three years. It was a very poverty stricken area. We did without many things, but did not care! When we really had to have something, God provided. Once, we needed tags for the car, and they cost three dollars. It was the deadline, but we did not have three <u>cents</u>! A preacher we knew was driving through town on the highway past our house. He stopped, came to the door, and handed me three dollars! He said God told him to stop and give us three dollars. I took it and said, "Thank you!"

When Robert came home, I explained and gave it to him, and he went and purchased the car tags!

Lutie Taylor, her husband, and the only daughter who was still living at home, began to come to our church even though they belonged to another church. Lutie and her daughter were very talented and helped out by playing the piano and singing specials.

We knew nothing about Robert's mom, Lutie's friendship, or the promise Lutie had made. One day she told me, and said she had kept that promise and had prayed many times for them over the years. Before Robert's dad died, he had come back to the Lord and gave it as his testimony. The siblings lived many years and had good times and many heartaches as we all do. They were very proud of their "baby brother", the preacher. They <u>all</u> eventually came to know the Lord!

One of the sisters had come to the altar after hearing Robert preach. She had cried, but went away saying she had sinned too much for God to forgive her, even though she was told God would forgive <u>all</u> our sins. Many years later she did go back to church, and was saved! A few years later she died, and at the funeral her pastor said he had never seen anyone else who was so happy and proud to <u>be</u> a Christian.

Never give up praying for your lost loved ones to be saved. It is worth it no matter how long it may take. God answered a mother's prayer even after she had passed on. Her faithful friend's prayers were answered who had kept her promise!

My Bucket List

Gayle Wilknson

When I was a teenager, long before the movie "The Bucket List" came out, I dreamed of some things I would like to do in my lifetime, but I was never really thinking I would get to do any of them. Here is my list:

1. Water ski
2. Snow ski
3. Go on a cruise
4. Go to Alaska
5. Go on an African safari

God's response to my "want to do" list.

1. I learned to water ski when I was still a teenager. The family of a young man I was dating had a boat and he taught me to ski.

2. When my son was 7, we went to Red River, New Mexico and learned to ski. We went many times after that.

3. I won my first cruise at my place of employment. I have been on many more since then.

4. On another cruise I went to Alaska.

5. This one I really didn't think would ever happen. But two years ago our church planned a mission trip to Africa. Even though I thought I might be too old to undertake such a trip, we made plans anyway. And while on the mission trip, we were taken to a wildlife reserve on a day and a half long safari! I saw all the animals in their own habitat: elephants, giraffes, zebras, lions, hippos, monkeys of all kinds, and many more. It was the highlight of my life.

God made it possible for me to accomplish all these things. And I have been privileged to see many other parts of this world. Every place one goes there is beauty indescribable. Our God truly is an awesome God.

*****

Prayer For My Mother When I Was Sixteen

When I was 16, my mother was very sick and the doctor came to our house to check on her. He told us that she probably wouldn't make it through it. As he said that, I flew out of the house to keep the people that were gathered around from seeing my sobbing.

I went outside and pleaded with God to let my mother live a while longer. I even put a number of years I needed into that prayer. I told God I needed to have my mother until I was at least 24 years old. I have no idea why I picked that particular number. I turned 25 on October 2, 1968, and my mother passed away on November 26, 1968.

God gave me exactly what I requested plus a little more. He let me get all the way through my 24th year, taking her at the beginning of my 25th year.

*****

Staph Infection

Shirley Miller

I have a testimony about my mother, Marie Miller. When I was about nine years old, my mother became very ill. Because of some very old fashioned teachings, (my mother was a relatively new Christian) she put off surgery.

She had been converted from being raised Catholic. I have nothing against Catholics. I believe some are very good Christians, and most are very good people.

She almost died and some relative talked her into going in and having surgery. She had a tumor in her womb and it had grown to the size of a grapefruit. The doctor and his nurse came to the house and took her to the hospital in El Campo,

Texas. Dr. Weinheimer was the surgeon. She went through the surgery but got worse and the doctor told my dad one evening that he wasn't sure if my mom would make it. He said it was a 50/50 chance.

I was staying with my aunt and uncle and I wanted to go home with my dad that night. My dad said "No, I have something important to do." I really thought he was being bad, but I also knew in my mind that he wanted to go home and pray. I must add that my dad was the kindest man I ever knew except his brother.

All his brothers and sisters were very kind. When I went to bed that night, I wept, but I did it silently. Another aunt stayed with my mother that night and they called the surgeon in to see my mother that evening.

He bent over her and asked "What's wrong. Mrs. Miller?"

At that moment....(this sounds really gross)....she threw up all over him!

It was gangrene! After that she began to improve. I've talked to RN's since then and told them that story. They told me that it was a miracle because they have never heard of anyone throwing up gangrene.

She lived to the age of 91 years old, and was a volunteer worker in church programs, and The Chamber of Commerce. She cooked and took food to people (some she didn't even know) but heard about. My dad never opposed her doing this. We always had plenty to eat.

She always gave God the credit and was a very active lady.

*****

God Supplied The Gas

Dilly Horne

I was living at home in Morton, Texas, in 1971, and working in Lubbock, about 60 miles away. I was working the night shift at Texas Instruments from four to twelve p.m. One night I came out to my car and someone had broken into my car and stole all my tapes and new school clothes I had just purchased.

I was so distracted that after I gave the police a report I left for home needing gas in my car. There were no gas stations open at that time of night in the edge of Lubbock or in the neighboring town of Levelland. I just kept driving and praying. There were no cell phones or any way to get a message to anyone if I did run out. So, I prayed God would keep me going. I drove through the outskirts of

Levelland, Whiteface, and still there were no open gas stations. The convenience store in Whiteface was only open from 7 to 11. Remember those days? None were open 24 hours.

I saw the sign for Morton and we lived on the near side of town and on the highway. Just as I drove into the yard, my car died. I had driven home, sixty miles, with the gas gauge showing empty! My dad had to put gas into the car's tank to start it the next morning!

God Met A Financial Need

Dilly Horne

Early on in our marriage, my husband and I had an unexpected bill come up for 150 dollars. It might have been medicine for the kids, or car repair. Whatever it was, it was important to us.

We knelt in our bedroom by the bed and

started praying for God to help us to find the money. There was a knock on the door, and I told my husband to keep on praying and I would answer the door.

It was an old friend I had not seen in ten years. She handed me a check and said, "I was passing through Lubbock and God told me to look you up in the phone book and give you a check for 150 dollars!" She hugged me and left.

I took the check and knelt by the bed and my husband. I slipped the check under his folded hands, he looked down, and tears came into his eyes. He looked at me in wonder, and I just nodded yes as we both cried.

It is important to note God had the answer on the way before we ever prayed! I have never seen her since! The old phrase of "Don't give up on the brink of a miracle!" was certainly true for us!

*****

Amazing, Bionic Power Jump to Safety

Ginny Hale

When I was around 35, I was a single mother living in Mesquite, and I worked for a developer off LBJ Freeway at Hillcrest in Dallas, Texas. Often on the way home I made it a habit to stop at Baily's Health Club to take an aerobics class or swim before going home.

During one class in particular, I felt especially nimble instead of exhausted. So, I decided to stop at a Tom Thumb grocery store to get a few things. I parked my car and headed towards the entrance. A man in an RV was having a heated argument with his wife. As I was approaching them, she got out and slammed the car door. Just as I stepped in front of the hood, he gunned his engine and slammed down the gas pedal with a screeching fast start.

At that very moment I was "bionically" lifted high into the air and propelled forward in a super extraordinary standing broad jump leap of more then 10 feet into the store entrance and landed like an Olympian with both feet squarely planted!

I have never done well in track in junior high; attempted broad jumps and landed not more than 3 feet forward and falling backward with one foot. But this power lifted super human jump was amazing to me! I felt exhilarated! People standing at the store entry doors, were amazed with mouths wide open at what they had seen. The man who gunned his engine was holding his chest with his hands; amazed, and gasping in disbelief at the potential carnage that had just been avoided.

It was just an extraordinary feat this bionic power jump that was beyond my ability! I was definitely carried, lifted in the hands of my guardian angels and pushed up and forward. I soared into the store like a kangaroo jump. I landed with joy and awe and with such force that I kept walking forward! I was elated to be alive! I was grateful to not be paralyzed, crushed, crippled, or a paraplegic and even dead under that RV. Immediately, I said, "Thank you Lord Jesus and ministering guardian angels for rescuing me!" I was rescued from the snare of the fowler; protected and kept safe and sound, by super human mighty intervention. I fully recognized it was the hand of my guardian angel who lifted me from danger and expertly planted my feet securely.

This amazing rescue made an indelible imprint and memory in my life that I continue to give God thanks for. The next day my calves were very sore and tight. Every step hurt. On my own I could never have leaped high and out of the way to safety in a flash of an instant.

This day I was aware of divine intervention. How amazing to realize I was watched over, guided, kept safe and sound, and closely guarded and provided for. My angels must have been with me in that aerobics class. It was a day I could have died at age 34 or never walked again.

It is true; He will give His angels charge over you. They watch over you to see and perform Gods' word and will for us! I am thankful now in my 60's to be so healthy, and active. I am still able to work out and I am kept safe as I drive and exercise. I am glad to be in the land of the living!

*****

Spain Adventure

Don Nevins

My wife used to work for a ceramic tile store in DeSoto, Texas, and she was selected to go on an all expense paid trip to Spain to see how they manufactured the products she was selling. I was able to go along with her, and my only expense was airfare for myself.

We arrived in Madrid and took a bus to the business place, and watched them manufacture tile from the sand to the slurry to forming to glazing to firing to packing. We also visited the furniture factory and watched fiberglass bathtubs and showers being manufactured.

One day we traveled up the coast for the best buffet lunch of fresh fish and everything else you could imagine. We visited the castle where the movie El Cid was filmed, along with other points of interest.

On our last day we were back in Madrid and had free time to go shopping and use up our local money. We stopped at McDonald's on the way back to the hotel, and Lorraine discovered her wallet was missing. At the hotel we reported it and were told, "I told you to be careful of pickpockets."

So, we went to the police station, and sat there a long time. I reached over and we joined hands and prayed. We asked God to have the wallet returned so we would not have to leave the country with this doubt hanging over our heads. Finally, another couple came in, and, with their help translating, we filled out a claim form. They were victims of a purse snatching. They had come to town to attend a wedding, and they were dressed to the "9's."

We took the form back to the hotel, and in a few minutes we were advised the wallet had been found, but it was in another town a few minutes away. I said, "Call a cab. We are going!"

When we arrived at the place, there were police walking around the car ahead of us carrying mirrors on a stick inspecting for bombs. We walked up to the gate, and two guys came carrying the wallet like it was a prized treasure. My wife looked through it and the thief had taken the small amount of money, about $8.00 American, a pad of blank checks, and a Visa card. They left the driver's license, social security card, Macy's, and other store cards.

Back at the hotel about two a.m. we were sitting in the lobby, and our guide, Raphael, came down the stairs. He was going to call his parents in Cuba, and wanted to know why we were up at that hour for he knew we were not part of the partying crowd. When we told him our story he said, "That is a miracle!" And it was.

When getting on the bus the next morning, we had an opportunity to tell the story to the group of about 32 people, and they also agreed it was a miracle.

I said I was not concerned about the checks because we were in another country, but one of the ladies said, no, and that she worked in a bank and those checks could always turn up.

We called Visa and canceled the card. When we got home we closed out the bank account, and went on with our lives. God protected us and it could have been much worse.

So, if you find yourself in a troubling situation the thing to do is pray. It works!

Mat: 18:19 "If two of you shall agree on earth as touching any thing that they shall ask, it shall be done for them of my Father which is in heaven, for where two or three are gathered together in my name, there am I in the midst of them." Jesus said, "Whatsoever you ask the Father in My Name it shall be done for you."

*****

The Red Buick Regal

Don Nevins

One SNOWY day when we lived in Red Oak and my wife worked in North Dallas off I-35 and Walnut Hill Road, she insisted she must go to work and I must drive her. So, we said a prayer and started out. The roads had been sanded and there was not much traffic. However, when we got to the intersection of I-35 and 183, the sand truck had gone down 183 and we turned North on I-35, bad situation, we did a 360 and my wife was speaking in tongues real loud!

Slam, crash, glass flying everywhere! We came to rest, actually bounced off a lady's car who had done the same thing, and was parked in the middle of the road. My driver side door hit her front fender. Nobody was hurt so we exchanged insurance information and we went on our way.

When we got to my wife's work place, some of the men saw us drive in with the driver side door hanging open, and they got a cardboard box and put a piece in the window and tied a rope to keep the door from flopping. I drove home with the heater going full blast.

Since this was our only car, something had to be done quickly. I prayed to the Lord to lead me to a door from a wrecking yard we could use. He did! It actually was from an Oldsmobile, the <u>same color</u>, but the trim strip, instead of being gold, was white and in a different location.

I borrowed my brother-in-law's van and picked it up for $160.00. I came home and removed the old door. The interior trim was different, and I had to change it out and install the automatic lock mechanism from the old door to the new. I stripped off the white trim strip and applied new gold tape, cleaned it up and *voila – i*t worked ! Well, almost, it would not close properly. I went to a body shop owned by a member of our Full Gospel Business Men's prayer group, and paid him $20.00 to adjust it.

For under $200.00 we got the door fixed and drove it till we traded it for a new car several years later. The insurance company was generous with the settlement, and we were able to catch up the payments in arrears at that time.

God is Good! All the time!

*****

God Watched Over Me

Keith Turner

While I was in the Air Force, I was stationed in Wichita Falls, Texas. It was close enough to the Dallas area for me to hitchhike home nearly every weekend.

I was blessed with rides and met several friendly people interested in helping a soldier in uniform.

One time I caught a ride with a group of soldiers which had been drinking pretty heavy. They wanted to go a different route than I usually took, and so I used it for an excuse to get out and try to catch another ride.

Shortly I caught a ride and we had only gone a few miles, and we saw where the carload of soldiers had hit a bridge and killed them all. God had watched over me!

How I Came To Know The Lord

Tayo Lancaster

At the age of 17 I lived in Jackson, Tennessee. A girl I wanted to go out with asked me to come and go to a revival with her. I went and listened to Ken Hall preach, and he was having a healing line.

A man came up in a wheelchair with a deformed leg. The knee was completely out of joint and the foot was turned almost backward. I was very interested to see what God was going to do for something so miraculous. I even told the Lord, "If you will heal that man's leg I will give my heart to you and serve you."

They prayed for the man and, as I watched, the knee went back into place, the foot straightened, and God miraculously healed him! I said to the

Lord, "That is good enough for me! Where do I sign?"

I gave my heart to God that night and ever since I have had a special anointing to pray for people with leg problems. I have prayed and God has lengthened legs on the spot. I prayed for one woman to have her leg lengthened and I was holding the wrong leg. She called out, "I don't want to be taller!" So, I prayed again and God made both legs the same.

Even in our Full Gospel Men's Group, I have been privileged to pray for one man which had an injury which left one leg shorter than the other and his pelvis out of adjustment which caused him great pain. God healed Bob Gibson and he has started back to walking and jogging and has not felt pain in his leg and pelvis since we prayed for him!

Back in Jackson, I later wanted to ask Ken Hall to come and have a little Bible study in my home. I had been thinking about asking him and I stopped at the four way stop where one way went to his house and one way continued on to mine. While I was praying for what to do I opened my eyes and I was sitting in his front driveway! I do not know how I got there! Not only that, he was coming out the door with two cups of coffee! He had been told by the Lord I was coming!

We sat on his front porch and made plans to start a Bible study in my home. We grew, and went to a small shopping center location. Then later a man gave him 25 acres along with some money, and he built a church. Today there is a good sized Church which started from the little Bible study in my home!

*****

The following is the testimonial from Bob Gibson, the man healed in our FGBMI (Full Gospel Business Men International) meeting.

~Editor

God Healed My Injured Leg

Bob Gibson

Thank the Lord that He is a healer! He has touched my body many times. I was in a FGBMI meeting with some brothers, and I was telling them of how my knees were from playing so much football. I found out that one of my legs was shorter than the other. In that meeting, Tayo Lancaster and the men prayed for me, and I tasted and saw that the Lord is good! I can stand here and say that God is a healer. He healed my leg and I will tell anyone who asks that God has healed me and is a healer.

Blind Baby Healed

Reverend Sam Farina

In 1996 I experienced a very unexpected miracle. On July 3 my father died and it was a very dark time of sorrow in my life. As I was leaving the hospital after his death, the pastor of First Assembly in Appleton called my cell phone. He insisted that I was to come to his church the next week to speak. As one can imagine, I was low in emotion after the death of my father and the funeral, but decided to go to the church for the multi day meeting.

Only a few minutes into the first meeting, a couple came forward with their baby boy who had been recently diagnosed as blind with no hope for a medical solution. They were holding the medical document from the doctors. I prayed for the baby boy. A week later the couple returned to the meeting holding the boy and a NEW medical document. They had noticed that the baby was tracking their movement after we prayed and decided to take the boy back to the doctor. Once there, the doctors declared that sight had been restored to the child.

I visited with the family two years ago and the boy still had perfect sight!

*****

Mission Trip To Poland

Dallas Horne

In July of 2002, I was on a mission trip to Poland. I had gone with a group of youth members from several churches in our area. While we were ministering in the streets of one of the cities we were in, I noticed a man standing to the side of the crowd of onlookers. As I looked at him, he and I caught eyes, and he approached me.

At first I was a little oblivious to what was actually going on. The man was noticeably drunk and grabbed me to give me a hug. I hugged him back, but was obviously fearful of him holding on to me. One of our leaders that was standing nearby saw the entire thing and said to me, "Rebuke it!"

As I was hugging this man, I began to pray for him. I asked in Jesus' name for him to be free of the bondages that were holding him. I remember rebuking the evil in his life. It was at that time that

I said, "In the name of Jesus!" He then released me from our hug. I looked at him in his eyes, and his total appearance and demeanor had changed.

He was clear eyed, and was able to focus on me. The man was TOTALLY sober! He then proceeded to hold out his hand. He had been holding on to a clear glass crack pipe. I watched as he threw the pipe to the side in some bushes. He then sat down on some steps that were behind us, and one of our translators, who was a member of the local church we were working with, sat and began to share the salvation message with him.

I watched as this man began to listen and agree with what was being said. At this time, we all were instructed that we had to leave. As we were walking away I turned to see that the man and the translator were still sitting on the steps talking.

That was when I began to weep. My heart was broken for this man. I cried for over an hour straight as we rode the bus to our next destination.

I could not get the man's face, and the miracle that God did through the Holy Spirit and me out of my mind. Finally, one of our leaders leaned over to me, hugged me, and said, "God is showing you His heart for the lost."

I believe that I felt the heart of God that day. It was burdened. I later found out that the Polish man came to the church that next week, and had given his heart to the Lord!

*****

Healing At Birth

Edgar Terrell

My grandparents have told me this many times. I was born at home so I could be close to my grandmother. It was out in the country around Snyder, Oklahoma, 24th day of July 1922.

Back then we didn't have screens on the doors or windows. It was a hot day. Some time after I had been born, my grandmother picked me up out of the bed, looked at me, and I had quit breathing. My heart had stopped, and I had turned blue in the face. My grandmother walked out on the front porch holding me. She was a godly Baptist woman. She looked into my face, prayed a prayer, breathed in to my face, and life came back into my body! I had been resuscitated!

The reason that I can stand here today, 89 years later, is because of a godly grandmother back then.

Later, I lived in Fort Worth. We moved there when I was about 15 from East Texas. My friend and I had gone down to the Fort Worth Stockyard area. There was a revival going on down by the courtyard, in the tabernacle. It was a Pentecostal meeting. It was the most exciting thing going on in North Fort Worth.

The pastor gave the invitation to come down to the altar. A man came over to me and asked, "Son, have you ever given your heart to the Lord?"

I told him, "No," and right there I gave my heart to the Lord. I went down to the front and made a public confession to make Jesus Christ my Lord and Savior.

*****

God Spoke To Me

Don Horne

My wife attended Southwestern Assemblies of God University in Waxahachie, Texas, for a year, and told our children often of her "adventures" in school.

She sang in Harvesters, a traveling chorale from the University. She talked about her best friend, Suzette, who was a twin. Suzette's sister would come visit and the house mother would check her sister in at "lights out" as present thinking it was her so she could stay out longer with friends which lived off campus.

The times my wife and her friends had experienced praying in the Holy Spirit for one another as they traveled; going to classes on a campus where every class began with a prayer; and the fun they had in the dorms made an impression on my girls to the point they wanted to attend school at SAGU. Of course, the idea of finding a Christian husband was, and I am sure still is, also a large consideration for some young women going to school in Waxahachie, a small town south of Dallas.

My oldest daughter, Suzette, (named for my wife's friend), went one year to a community school in Houston, and another to South Plains College in Levelland, Texas, to be near her grandmother.

When Monika graduated high school two years after Suzette, the two girls worked, saved their money, and wanted to go to SAGU together. We applied for Pell Grants and other forms of college funding and believed we had the financing all in place.

We received the dorm assignments and acceptance from the University, took the girls to school, and settled them in their room on a Sunday. Just as we got back to Houston the phone rang and the girls were in tears. Their funding was not complete. They were going to be allowed to spend the night in the dorm, but the next day, if the money did not appear in the main computer, they would have to move out. We all were devastated.

We went to church that evening, but I did not go in the building. I sat in the car and prayed. We had done everything correct, I thought, to fill out all the forms and the numerous documents for my girls to go to school.

After the service, my wife and I went home and into the girls' room and knelt beside one of the beds and continued praying. My wife went on to bed, and I lay there crying and praying in the Spirit until, finally, I was prayed out and quiet. I heard a still voice say to me gently, *"What do you want me to do for you?"* Even though I had never heard Him speak to me audibly before, I knew the voice of my Master!

I knew I was in His presence and could have whatever I asked. Similar to being told I could have only one wish, I thought about all the things I knew I could have: money, car, home, etc. The truth is, I said, with a humble heart, "God, take care of my girls' financial needs for college, and let me think about the rest for a moment." I suppose it does not sound spiritual to put God "on hold," but I am emphasizing how careful I was about responding. Knowing I had, for an instant, the ear of God, I did not want to miss the opportunity. Interestingly, I started crying again and told Him, "I want your wisdom and knowledge." I knew, and still know, without Him I have nothing.

I went to sleep in peace. The next morning about eight the phone rang and the girls were almost yelling in their excitement, "We got in! The rest of our finances came in during the night!" My wife had to hang up the phone as I was crying again and thanking God for answering my prayer. I suppose I do cry a lot for a man. I am moved to tears for everything from people's testimonials to the score of the latest Dallas Cowboy game!

Since that night God has given me an insight and hunger for the scriptures like I never had before. When I read the Bible at times before, the "Spirit of Sleep" seemed to come, and I could not read for very long in the night time without nodding off. I can read the Bible now, look up at the time, and realize I have been reading for hours!

Both girls, Suzette and Monika, and my son, Dallas, have graduated from Southwestern Assemblies of God University in Waxahachie. They all are married and serving the Lord today.

Suzette was probably too picky, but Monika did find a young man for a husband on a missionary flight to England from the University. She knew him from school, but he had an "afro", a beard, and a couple of tattoos. She had not thought about him seriously as even a friend until she sat for several hours and talked with him on the plane to England and back.

His dad and mother, Lavon and Mike Bray, are wonderful servants of God, and she found he was a lot deeper spiritually than she had believed. He asked if he could call her when they returned to school, but she was surprised when he actually did a few days later.

They began dating and they now have been married for ten years, and have two beautiful daughters, Cali and London. London was named for the destination of the trip where her parents met. I am so thankful they did not meet on a trip to Albuquerque or some other exotic city!

The girls did not raise enough money for both of them to go to England. So, Suzette gave up her seat on the plane and went to minister on the streets of Los Angeles, California, with a group of her friends. Monika may not have become friends with Lance, her husband, if she had not been on the plane to England!

*****

Answers To Prayers In Sunday School Class

Don Horne

In 1985 my wife and I were co-teaching a Sunday School class in Slaton, Texas, which is just outside of Lubbock. I was the Assistant Manager of the Anthony's Department Store, and my wife was a kindergarten teacher.

We were teaching a unit on "Answers to Prayer." We went over Biblical references to

128

answered prayer, and I also used other reference books for how to pray and get God to answer.

At the end of the series of lessons I asked the group of adults, "If you knew you had the ear of God, you were in His presence, and you could have anything you want what would you ask?"

I went around the room, and, when we thought about what we would actually and honestly desire from God if we were in His presence, there was a universal answer. We all said we wanted more of God and to know His ways. We found it interesting not one of us would ask for needs outside of the Spiritual Realm!

One couple was praying about a son living in Dallas which was away from the Lord. Another couple were having marital problems. A woman named Helen Lee wanted to receive the Baptism of the Holy Spirit with the evidence of speaking in tongues. I wanted direction in my job for I had an offer in another town. None of us would have asked God for the answer to those needs. We would have asked for more of Him.

I told the class, "Then, let's just praise God before we go out to the main service. Don't ask Him for anything, but just praise Him as if we had already received the answer." We praised Him for a few minutes, and then went out of our room to the main service.

It was the order of service in that church to have prayer at the altar before the church service began. Our little group went to the altar and began praying. I felt a direction from the Lord to lay hands on Helen Lee and help her pray for the Baptism. She had been seeking earnestly for over 20 years. As soon as I laid my hands on her, she raised her arms and hands and started speaking in tongues for the first time in her life!

The next Sunday, the couple with the wayward son told us, as they entered the house from church, the telephone was ringing, and it was their son who wanted them to know he went to church that morning and gave his heart to the Lord! The couple having marital problems were holding hands and telling us they were to leave on a cruise the next week! Although it meant a move to Lubbock, I worked for another store, and it was a great job until the company was bought out and closed. The direction I was seeking sent us to Houston where all three children received the Baptism, graduated from the same high school, and went to college together.

The three of them graduated from SAGU. They are married, and we all now live close to one another in the Dallas area. God answered our needs when we sought Him in praise!

The following is a very special addendum to this book which came my way from a special lady in our class, and I am humbly including it in the revised edition.

~Don Horne, Editor

My Life

Berna Mae (Robison) Pruett

I grew up in an Assembly of God Minister's Home. I was born in Texas, and I had wonderful parents who loved and served the Lord faithfully. I also lived my growing up years in Texas. I attended Southwestern Bible Institute in my Junior and Senior years of High School. At Southwestern, I became acquainted with Dick Pruett, who grew up in Corpus Christi, Texas. We were married in November of 1951. We were invited to become an

Assistant Pastor in the City of Pampa, Texas and began our Ministry there in January of 1952 at the First Assembly of God Church. In those early years, we ministered in Texas, then our ministry took us to California two different times. Finally, in the late 60's we moved there again and this time stayed 17 years in full time Ministry.

We had a really fine, loving, enjoyable marriage. Dick always treated me so very special. We sang together in church, directed choir, and put together Trio's and Quartets. I played the piano and Dick always included me in the Ministry Pattern. He was a very fine man, husband, father, and was liked by everyone. Ministry was his life and God used him in so many ways. He was an astute preacher of the Word. He could take control well, always had lots of great ideas, and being a director was very natural for him

We have five wonderful children.....four daughters and one son. Now I also have two sons-in-law, and one daughter-in-law. I have eight grandchildren, four grandchildren in-law and two great grandsons. It is a wonderful, close, enjoyable, fun loving family. I couldn't enjoy them more.

This is my Testimony of God's Love and Grace through the years.

In 1976, my husband of 25 years began to have problems with his eye sight caused by his Diabetes condition. In 1979, a few days before his 50th birthday, he woke up one morning and could not see his face in the mirror. This began a whole new way of life for him and for me. For a man always in charge of everything.....this was really a difficult time. Of course, I had to take over responsibilities that had always been his and be sure that he did not feel like a "nobody"! It was a very traumatic time for us both. But God.....our wonderful Lord.... was always right there to guide and assure us of His presence and control. Dick experienced many conversations with the Lord, and God gave him so many words of encouragement. One of them was, *"Give me the brokenness of your life and I will touch hundreds and even thousands of others who are broken in some area of their life and I will restore them"*.

He was well known in the Southern California Assemblies of God because he had served in the District Office as Christian Education Director. So, when Pastors became aware of his situation, they began to call and ask him to speak to their congregations. They needed his POSITIVE word to their people in need. God gave him a wonderful message of hope and the ability to deliver it without 6 pages of notes, which of course, was a new experience for him.

And, during all these new ways in our lives, I personally sensed the Lord so near to me. In the many times when I really did not know what tomorrow would bring, and actually did not know what the next hour could bring, such a peace flooded over me that could only come from our

Lord. At one point when I was feeling troubled, the Lord led me to read a scripture in the Bible. Proverbs, chapter 3, verses 5 & 6:

"Trust in the Lord with all thine heart, and lean not unto thine own understanding. In all thy ways acknowledge Him, and He shall direct thy paths." As I was reading this, He was also giving me a "tune" that seemed to fit with the words of the scripture. I went to the piano and began to play the notes I was hearing and then as I added the words I realized that He had actually given me a song to sing! What a wonderful experience! The words of the scripture were guiding me to trust Him and that He was directing me! I did, and I have, and He has never ever failed me.

We were invited to Texas in late 1983 to Minister in various Churches, and upon visiting our 'ole Alma Mater, Southwestern Assemblies of God College, we reconnected with Alumni and Friends of the past. One day after arriving back home in California, we received a phone call from Dr. Dick Guynes, the President of Southwestern. He and Dick had been students there in the late '40's.

He said, "Dick, the Lord has been talking to me and I feel that you are supposed to be here at Southwestern as our Campus Pastor." What a shock! Asking someone who is blind to be Campus Pastor? Move back to Texas.....leaving our children in California....could this really be the thing to do at this point of our life? Well, we began to have our own conversation with the Lord....made a trip back to Texas....and felt that it really was the Lord's will for us. So, in May of 1984, we and our son moved to Waxahachie, Texas, to fill the position of Campus Pastor, and our son would attend college. It was a tremendous experience for each of us. The Lord began immediately to use both of us on a daily basis. We made all the arrangements for the Chapel Services each day, and, Dick, as pastor, led the service. We arranged for special music and speakers. I am thankful how the Lord used me also in so many ways in the midst of the greatest trauma of our lives.

I enjoyed all the responsibilities, and the contact with people was such a great blessing. Because Dick needed me to prepare him for each day, the Lord was using me in ways that I had never imagined. Yes, the Lord's strength for me was moment to moment, and He never failed to be there in every situation that would occur.

In Feb of '85, Dick had kidney failure and was placed on dialysis 3 days per week. This was another great responsibility for me, and so difficult for him physically. But he kept going.....never missing a day at the College. November 30th of that year we celebrated our 34th wedding anniversary. Three days later, on December 2nd, Dick woke up that morning saying, "I don't feel good." That was the day that the Lord took him home to Heaven. It was something we had always known could happen, but, it was quite a shock to realize "this was the day."

So, after his Memorial Services and burial, again, my life is taking on another new phase. Yes, I am lonely and miss him so very much, but I am also very comforted to realize that he is now out of pain. He is seeing all his loved ones in Heaven, and enjoying his new home. He knows that the Lord will continue to take care of me. Yes, and He has! God is SO FAITHFUL!

When the College hired us, they had salaried me so that we could keep Dick's disability income. We did not realize at the time that it would be a tremendous help for me when his time would come. So, since I was the employed one, I continued with all our responsibilities each day. I was so glad to have my Son here with me. I was not at home alone. He understood what I was going through, and we had a great relationship. My daughters were also very near me too, even though they were miles away. They were so loving and attentive to my needs, and always there when I needed them.

Of Course, I had many questions about what the future would hold for me without Dick. Like......should I go back to California where my daughters still lived, and where Dick and I had so many personal friends?

Lord, "What does the future hold?" was my greatest question. So, time passed, and the Board met in February and asked me to stay on and continue with the responsibilities that we had been given in the beginning. It was awesome to realize the Lord really was looking after me, as He had promised. This was beyond anything I had ever imagined. This was such a tremendous blessing, to continue to be here where we had been together and enjoy all the students that I meet each year.....WHAT A BLESSING.

That was 26 years ago and I am still employed at Southwestern...now a University.....and could not ask for a more wonderful place to be and to have been all these years. I have come to know so many students....made friends with Faculty and Staff through the years.....get to hear from and see Alumni I attended Southwestern with. It is the greatest Blessing the Lord could have ever allowed me to experience. I will never stop praising Him for his faithfulness to me. I realize He had my life planned from the beginning, and each experience was in His Hands to bring me to where I am today. THANK YOU LORD!

I want each of you to know that just as the Lord had my life in His hands all the way.....you too can expect that He is leading and planning your life each day that you serve Him. We can make preparations daily, and should, but God has His plan for us and it is so wonderful to know that HE IS IN CHARGE. Always know whatever your situation is...you can, and must always, *"Trust in the Lord with all your heart and lean not unto thine own understanding. In all thy ways acknowledge Him and He shall direct thy paths."*

So, remain faithful and experience God's blessings on your life. Again I say, "HE IS FAITHFUL!"

Demanded For Trial

Reverend Richard (Dick) Pruett

*"**DEMANDED FOR TRIAL**" was the final sermon preached by Reverend Richard Pruett, only eight days before his death. This moving sermon/testimony was ministered to the congregation of the Calvary Assembly of God Church, Waco, Texas, during the Sunday evening service, on November 26, 1985.*

This special sermon/testimony is dedicated to those going through a time of "trial and testing" in their lives.

I know there is a teaching abroad in our world Christians should not have too many problems; they can confess away their problems, and through confession, everything will be righted...confessing a Cadillac in every garage...just name it and it is yours...it is just a matter of the right confession...the right thought pattern! Anyone who lives beneath that axiom is living beneath his or her privileges, and is walking out of tune with God's will for their lives. BUT, HEAR ME! That is not true to the scriptures, nor is it true to the experience of life.

Jesus said in John's Gospel, chapter 16, *"For in this world ye shall have tribulation but be of good cheer, I have overcome the world."* Sounds like we could have a few problems! And speaking through the lips of James... *"count it all joy when you fall into divers temptations (tests or trials) knowing this; that the trial of your faith worketh patience, and let patience have her perfect work that you may be mature, wanting nothing."*

Yes, it is true we can bring certain circumstances on ourselves, but when our hearts are clean before God and we find ourselves in a valley experience, it is for a purpose. God has something He is working out in our lives. First Peter, chapter 5, verse 10... *"After that ye have suffered a while, make you perfect, stablish, strengthen, settle you.*" So, these are the reasons that difficulties come to us the children of God.

In 1976, I lost the sight in my right eye after having three laser operations performed by one of the finest surgeons in Southern California. Three years later, in 1979, two days after my wife, Berna, and I came home from a vacation in Hawaii, I woke up and could not see anything. I could not see my hand in front of my face. I was later declared legally blind by the State of California. Needless to say, this was very traumatic for me. I despaired for my life, wondering what I was going to do! I had a son to finish raising and get through college. All my hopes, dreams, and aspirations came crashing and crumbling around me.

To add to my despair, we had a gentleman in our church who sent word to me by one of the staff pastors, to "tell Pastor Pruitt to get the sin out of his life and God will heal him." I did not need to take a guilt trip like that...yet, I did! I took the trip and wondered, "GOD WHAT KIND OF SIN COULD I HAVE COMMITTED THAT WOULD CAUSE SUCH A TRAGEDY TO HAPPEN TO ME? WAS IT MY SIN, OR WAS IT THE SIN OF MY PARENTS?"

I began to wake up at 2:00 and 3:00 in the morning, stumbling out of the bedroom into the living room and falling into a chair or couch, weeping my heart out, asking God to please reveal the sin that I might have committed to cause such a tragedy in my life. Never will I forget, though I could not see my hand in front of my face, on one of those early hour experiences, the room brightly lit up with the Shekinah glory of God. You will know when you are in God's presence! I sensed arms go about my body. Whether they were the arms of an angel, or the Lord Himself, I really don't know, but at that moment I heard Him whisper to me, *"There was nothing between my soul and the Saviour, and soon I would know something of His dealings with me in my life."*

So, I kept putting one foot in front of the other, and kept walking with God, knowing that He would reveal Himself to me in the course of time. On one of those mornings, I tuned to channel 30 in Los Angeles to listen to the DOMATA SERIES (which means "God's gifts to men").

I listened to a young man who captured my attention as he began to talk about the KAIROS TIMES OF LIFE, or the various "seasons of life" that come to a child of God. He quoted the words of Jesus from the book of Luke, chapter 22, verse 31. *"Simon, Simon, behold Satan hath desired to have you that he may sift you as wheat, but I have prayed for you that your faith fail not and when thou art converted, strengthen the brethren."*

As I listened the speaker said, "It is more meaningful than the King James Version that we have at our disposal today. What Jesus literally said to Peter was: *"Simon, Simon, Satan hath demanded you for trial that he might make a sieve out of you; that he might show up the chaff of your life; that he can prove to those around you that you are not a follower of Mine. He wants to show up the inconsistencies of your life, Peter, but I have prayed for you...literally, I AM praying for you.*"

May I suggest to you, Christian, the prayer for Peter was more than a good-night prayer like, "lay me down to sleep." The original language was, "I am agonizing for you, Peter. I am interceding for you, that your faith fail not in this KAIROS (uncertain) or particular season of your life. And when you are converted or changed, after much twisting and turning, then you will be able to minister to those who have problems in their lives."

You know, there is something about the authority structure of God that Satan, who is the adversary of mankind, still has the privilege to stand before God and accuse the brethren. He is known as the "accuser," and demands God's children for "trial." I have read in the Bible that Satan is as a *"roaring lion, going about seeking whom he may devour."* You see, it is not until the book of Revelations that he is dehorned and dethroned; put into the pit, and ultimately into the Lake of Fire, and until then, we <u>do</u> have an adversary who as a roaring lion goes about seeking whom he may devour.

BUT HEAR ME! There is another Lion loose in the world, and He is the Lion of the tribe of Judah! He is sitting at the right hand of the Father. His present ministry is that of being an <u>advocate</u>, praying for your cause and mine into the ears of the Heavenly Father, and He prays with the same intensity as when He prayed for Peter. His plan is that we are to be VICTORIOUS IN EVERY CIRCUMSTANCE IN WHICH WE FIND OURSELVES.

Yes'm **DEMANDED FOR TRIAL!** Let me suggest that the apostle Peter was not the only person in God's book who was demanded for trial. Job was "demanded for trial." He lost his wealth, his health, and all his children. But, because he remained true to God through his trying time...he did not regard iniquity in his heart nor did he charge God falsely...just read the last chapter of Job and see where God blessed him with greater wealth, greater health, and the same number of children filled his home. *"Though God slay me, yet will I trust Him...when He has tried me, I will come forth as pure Gold, tried in the fire."* HEAR ME, that sounds like a man who has victory in his life! He proved true in the dark circumstance of life.

Also, there were three Hebrew lads, Shadrach, Meschach, and Abednego. Their being "demanded for trial" took on another form..."the fiery furnace." It was heated seven times its normal heat, they were bound with new cords and thrown into the furnace because they would not bow their knees to some dumb image the king

Nebuchadnezzar had erected.

The first thing that happened was a liberating experience, because all the cords were burned off! But, greater than this, was the privilege of walking with the fourth man, "who was like the Son of God." I wonder if we fail to realize in our fiery furnace experience that we are walking with the fourth man and He has promised to never leave us, even in the midst of the storm. His promise is, *"Fear not, for I have redeemed thee. I have called thee by name; thou art Mine. When thou passed through the fire thou shalt not be burned."* You will be like the Hebrew children, you will not even have the smell of smoke on you. If you will follow the life of each of the Apostles, they were, on some occasion in their lives, **DEMANDED FOR TRIAL.**

Let me share with you my personal testimony! As I stated, it was in 1976 I lost the sight in my right eye. Just three years later, I lost the sight in my left eye and was then declared legally blind. It was a traumatic time, and yet not all of life was down hill. I attended The Braille Institute in Los Angeles, learning Braille and studying psychology and typing.

These things kept me busy. I had a whole new way of life to learn. It was the month of September again. (I think I am going to skip the month of September from now on, for they are a little treacherous!) My brother Bob, pastor of our church, was preaching on Paul's thorn in the flesh...how Paul had to make peace with that circumstance in his life before God could use him, and before he could resume his walk in the Lord. I was not buying it for a minute. I was tossing it over to the person behind me!

A "root" of bitterness had crept into my heart and I was beginning to resist what God was trying to do in my life. We left the church that day and Berna and I went to a nearby Cafe to eat our noon meal. We went through the line, sat down, mumbled a word of thanks, but I could not eat. I began to empty the bitterness and resistance and the unfairness of it all.

I thought of the life of Job and his problems that lasted only about nine months before he was on his way out of the valley, and I said, "GOD THIS HAS BEEN A YEAR AND ENOUGH IS TOO MUCH!" I could hear my wife softly weeping across the table. I thought, "How unfair," for it was she who put her arms around me and said, "We are going to make it through." It was she who read the scriptures to me over and over again, and taught me to eat off a plate I could not see; to dress myself, and to get back and forth to the church. So I apologized to her and we ate in silence.

At the close of the meal, I said I was going to walk home. (I had walked before, first with someone, and then alone.) She took the car and went home. I knew I had to hear from God! So, I took my white cane and began to tap my way along the Pacific Coast Highway in Lomita, California. I might have walked a block and a half when I heard a voice speaking to me.

I am not one to hear voices ordinarily. The voice said to me, "WHAT DO YOU HAVE IN YOUR HAND?"

I instinctively turned to my left because it was the direction the voice was coming from. Then, I stopped and waited. I thought surely someone would come and talk with me. When no one came, I turned and resumed tapping my way down the street.

I heard the voice again, "WHAT DO YOU HAVE IN YOUR HAND?" Immediately the Holy Spirit took me to another person in the Bible who was asked the very same question...Moses, after he had spent 40 years on the back side of the desert.

God began to speak to the heart of Moses saying, "I am not through with you yet. I have a job I want you to do." Moses began to make excuses as to how incapable he was such as an impediment of speech, but God already knew all that!

When God asked, "What do you have in your hand?" Moses said, "It is a rod."

God said, "Throw it down," and it became a serpent! The Bible says Moses was afraid of snakes and took off running!

"Pick it up by the tail, Moses," said God. He did and it became a rod again. God was simply saying to Moses, "It is ME, and I am not through with you. I have something more for you to do...this is not the back side of the desert anymore. I am ready for you to do My work in Israel." Moses submitted to the voice of the Lord.

As quickly as that story flashed through my mind, the Holy Spirit took me back again to a young stripling of a man on the back side of his father's farm, taking care of the ewe lambs. David was sent down also to take food to his brothers to see how the battle was faring against the

Philistines. There he faced an impossible confrontation with a giant, who was shouting threats to Israel. Goliath was his name. Offended he would disrespect the God of Israel, he took five stones and stood on the battlefield willing to give God all he had.

David did not possess the armor of Saul or his weapons of warfare, but he had the testimony of something he had proven in the past and he gave it to God. What he had was just a little slingshot and some stones. He went out and God gave the battle to David and to Israel.

One more story flashed through my mind and that one was from Matthew's Gospel about a little boy with five loaves and two fishes and the question was asked, "WHAT ARE THEY AMONG SO MANY?" Yet, the boy was willing to give what he had to Jesus. Jesus was willing to receive them! He took the loaves and the fishes, blessed them, and fed the multitude numbering five thousand men, besides the women and children. After they ate, twelve basketfuls of the fragments were gathered!

I shall never forget the sound of that voice saying, "What do you have in your hand?" I knew I had to get home or they might put me into Harbor General Hospital in a strait jacket for weeping as I was before God. I realized God was dealing with me for He had something for me to do. It was there I had a prayer meeting and made a new commitment to God.

I thought I would never be able to preach the Gospel again. After all, I could not go to the pulpit without six to ten pages of notes and here I was blind. I made a commitment to God, "I will follow you."

The Lord said, "GIVE ME THE BROKENNESS OF YOUR LIFE."

I said, "Lord, you can have all of my life; my eyes, my whole frame for the rest of my days, and I will take every opportunity I have to share the claims of Christ to a world without God."

God answered, "GIVE ME THE BROKENNESS OF YOUR LIFE, AND I WILL USE IT TO TOUCH HUNDREDS AND THOUSANDS OF OTHERS WHO ARE BROKEN IN SOME AREA OF THEIR LIFE, AND I WILL RESTORE THEM!" That commitment has lasted six years now. I thank God for his goodness and grace in my life.

I know that some of you are hurting in some area of your life, or the Lord would not have awakened me this morning at 2:30 to pray for you and hold you up in prayer. I have asked God to touch you where you may be **"DEMANDED FOR TRIAL."** It may be in the area of relationships or in the area of finances. It may be in the area of physical that God would touch you and make you whole.

You may ask, "Do you believe in healing?"

I absolutely do, more than I ever have in my

life...I believe in it. That is one of the areas the adversary wanted to defeat me; no one would want me to pray for them. I made a commitment that very day to pray for people, and God has been so gracious to heal, touch, and make whole.

If in some area of your life you are **"DEMANDED FOR TRIAL,"** know this...GOD LOVES YOU AND WITH A MILLION FLUID ARMS HE REACHES AROUND YOU! I want these arms to go about your life, to feel Him drawing you to Himself and to hear him whisper, "I love you. Even in the midst of the storm, I have victory for you and will bring you out!"

From The Author/Editor

This book has become a "labor of love" for me. I have been reminded of the awesome power of God at work in my life and the lives of my friends. It has forced me to look at my own faith, and how I have been relating to God. There is nothing too hard, or impossible, with our heavenly Father.

I smile when I hear people say they do not believe in God Jehovah. The truth is, Jehovah has existed from the beginning, and will to the end of eternity. You can reject Him, but you have to believe He exists to be able to do so. Knowing God exists, why won't you accept Him? He believed in <u>you</u> enough to send His only begotten Son that you might be reconciled to Him. He is waiting for you to come home, Prodigal. There are similar testimonies of God's love and provision waiting for you to write. What are you waiting for?

~Don Horne